D0649580

L. E. SMOOT MEMORIAL LIBRARY
9533 KINGS HIGHWAY
KING GEORGE, VA 22485

AIRCRAFT

Air Show Pilots and Airplanes

Timothy R. Gaffney

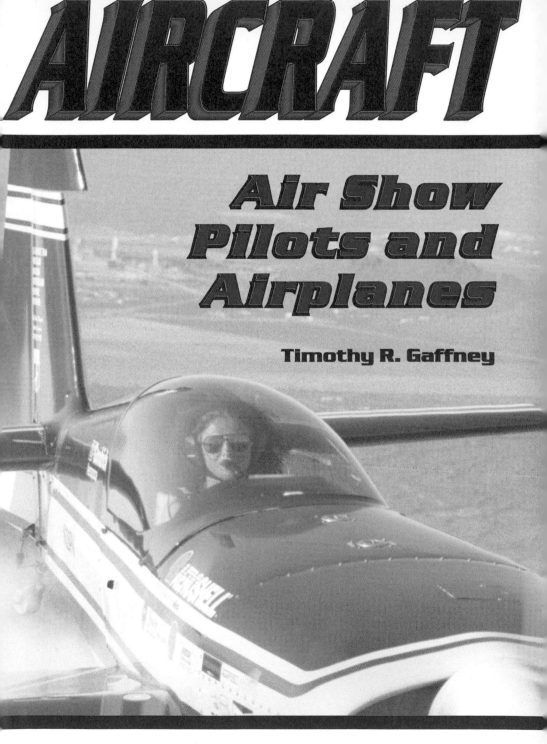

Enslow Publishers, Inc.
40 Industrial Road PO Box 38
Box 398 Aldershot
Berkeley Heights, NJ 07922 Hants GU12 6BP
USA UK

http://www.enslow.com

L. E. SMART MEMORIAL LIBRARY
9533 KINGS HIGHWAY
KING GEORGE, VA 22485

To the memory of Bruce Baty
Air show announcer, mentor, friend

Copyright © 2001 by Timothy R. Gaffney

All rights reserved.

No part of this book may be reproduced by any means
without the written permission of the publisher.

Library of Congress Cataloging-in-Publication Data

Gaffney, Timothy R.
    Air show pilots and airplanes / Timothy R. Gaffney
        p. cm. — (Aircraft)
    Includes bibliographical references (p.) and index.
    ISBN 0-7660-1570-X
    1. Air shows—Juvenile literature. 2. Stunt flying—Juvenile literature.
    3. Airplanes—Juvenile literature. 4. Air pilots—Juvenile literature.
    [1. Air shows. 2. Stunt flying. 3. Airplanes. 4. Air pilots.]
    I. Title. II. Series: Aircraft (Berkeley Heights, N.J.)
    TL506.A1G34 2001
    629.13'074—dc21

                                               00-010125

Printed in the United States of America

10 9 8 7 6 5 4 3 2 1

To Our Readers: We have done our best to make sure all Internet Addresses in this
book were active and appropriate when we went to press. However, the author
and the publisher have no control over and assume no liability for the material
available on those Internet sites or on other Web sites they may link to. Any
comments or suggestions can be sent by e-mail to comments@enslow.com or
to the address on the back cover.

Photo Credits: Timothy R. Gaffney

Cover Photo: Timothy R. Gaffney

Contents

CHAPTER 1

Strap In!

Patty Wagstaff's Extra 300S

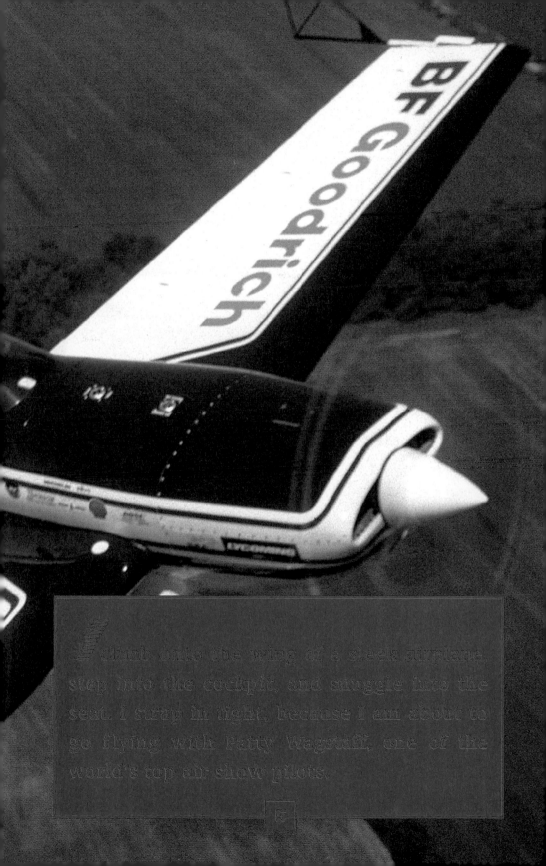

I climb onto the wing of a sleek airplane, step into the cockpit, and snuggle into the seat. I strap in tight, because I am about to go flying with Patty Wagstaff, one of the world's top air show pilots.

Wagstaff checks my harness and cinches it even tighter, until it almost hurts. Then she climbs into the backseat and straps herself in. She closes the long, clear canopy over our heads.

Wagstaff has borrowed this two-seat airplane, an Extra 300L, to give me a taste of air show flying. Her own plane, an Extra 300XS, has only one seat. Otherwise, the two are much alike: small, slender, and built for action.

The cockpit is snug. I am surrounded by a framework of metal tubes with a panel of gauges before me. There is a control stick between my knees, and a throttle lever by my left knee. Wagstaff has the same controls in her cockpit. The canopy is so clear that I touch it to make sure it is there.

The engine buzzes to life. The propeller on the nose spins into a blur. The airplane rolls lightly as Wagstaff taxis it to the runway. The engine's buzz grows into a roar. The plane sprints down the runway. Before I know it, we are airborne. The ground seems to drop away as we rise smoothly into a clear blue sky.

The flying that air show pilots do is called aerobatic flight. Aerobatic flight involves loops, rolls, spins, and other wild maneuvers never experienced on an ordinary flight. Air show pilots play in the sky, leaping and diving like dolphins in the sea. But it is a serious form of play, because they push their airplanes, and themselves, to the limits of their abilities.

The cockpit of Patty Wagstaff's Extra 300XS is made of a tough, tubular framework. Notice the windows in the floor and the straps of her harness.

≡ Sudden, Furious, Precise

The airplane snaps suddenly into a bank to the left. Wagstaff is banking the plane to turn. She snaps it back and we are level again. This is not like flying on an airliner, where every maneuver is smooth and gentle. Snap! Snap! Wagstaff's movements are quick and crisp. Her air show flying is the same way: sudden, furious, and precise.

Wagstaff hauls back on the control stick and pulls the plane into a loop. Up, up, and back we go, carving a big O in the sky. This is known as an inside loop: Our heads are inside the O. The plane pulls us with it against the force of gravity, just like an elevator when it starts to go up— only much harder and faster.

In an inside loop, the acceleration makes you feel as if a big weight is pushing down on you. I feel myself being squashed into my seat. It makes me feel right side up, even as the plane loops up and back until it is upside down. I look "up" where it seems the sky should be and see the ground instead.

Wagstaff completes the loop. Next, she pushes the stick forward. The plane dives into an outside loop. This time, our heads are outside the O. Down and under we go until we are upside down at the bottom of the loop, then back up and over. This time I am being pushed out from my seat. My safety harness bites into my shoulders and legs, but I am glad it is tight: It is all that holds me inside the plane.

Then come the tumbles. Wagstaff flips the plane end over end. The plane yanks me hard one way, then another. Brown earth, blue sky, and blazing sun swirl crazily around us.

"How are you feeling?" Wagstaff asks. Her voice sounds light and happy in my headset. She flies like this every day. But I wonder if my stomach can take another flip, and I say so.

Wagstaff laughs, but she understands. She levels out and heads back to the airport while my stomach slowly settles down.

She makes one final pass down the runway—upside down. I look "up" and see the gray runway pavement

Patty Wagstaff is about to cut the ribbon with her inverted Extra 300XS at AirVenture 99 in Oshkosh, Wisconsin.

streaming by at racecar speed. I clutch the sides of my seat, sure my head is about to scrape the ground. But Wagstaff is in complete control.[1]

≡ Dazzling the Crowds

Every year from March through November, Wagstaff and her Extra 300XS dazzle crowds at air shows around the United States. Wagstaff is one of the world's best aerobatic pilots, and her Extra 300XS is one of the world's best aerobatic airplanes. Together, they do things that look impossible.

Air shows began at the dawn of flight, when airplane builders hired pilots to show off their machines to the public. From 1911 until his death in 1915, Lincoln Beachey thrilled Americans from coast to coast with death-defying stunts. He became the first American to loop the loop, one after another, as well as the first man to fly upside down. He even picked a handkerchief off the ground with his wing tip. He named his airplane the Little Looper.[2]

After World War I, the U.S. Army sold off training airplanes it no longer needed. In the early 1920s, some pilots bought the planes and flew from town to town, selling rides and performing stunts. They became known as barnstormers.

"These planes were oftentimes not in the greatest shape and came apart, killing the pilot and passengers," said Dave Weiman, editor and publisher of *World Airshow News*. Air accidents caused the federal government to

Fans watch Wagstaff's air show performance at sunset.

start regulating airplanes and pilots. Aviation events became safer and better organized.[3]

Today, communities around the United States and in other countries put on hundreds of weekend air shows every year. Air shows attract between 15 million and 18 million people every year in more than 450 communities in the United States and Canada, said John Cudahy, president of the International Council of Air Shows. Air shows, he said, are "one of the top five spectator businesses on the [North American] continent."[4]

Today's air shows have the old-fashioned air of a carnival, with food booths and souvenir stands. At some

The U.S. Air Force Thunderbirds prepare to fly at the 1999 United States Air and Trade Show in Dayton, Ohio. The biggest shows schedule the best pilots and military jet teams.

shows, military and commercial airplanes are parked on display while the flying acts twirl before the crowd. The biggest shows schedule the best pilots and military jet teams, such as the U.S. Air Force Thunderbirds and the U.S. Navy Blue Angels.

Today's shows are still a lot like the early shows—noisy, exciting, and busy with what look like death-defying stunts. The difference is that air show flying today is a highly developed activity. Pilots now practice long and hard in specially designed and built airplanes. They balance the risky nature of their flying with high-quality machinery and razor-sharp skills.

CHAPTER 2

Rock-and-Roll Flying

Just resting on its landing gear, Patty Wagstaff's Extra 300XS looks like it wants to fly. Its body is long and low. Its tail is close to the ground and rests on a small tail wheel. Its nose is angled toward the sky. It is easy to walk up to the side of Wagstaff's plane and peek into the cockpit through its bubble canopy.

Two more windows are in the bottom of the plane, near where the pilot's feet go. Floor windows help aerobatic pilots see in all directions, so they can keep their bearings as they twirl in the sky.

Wagstaff's plane is not made for long-distance flying or for carrying much besides the pilot, fuel, and a small tank of

The body of the Extra 300XS is long and low. The tail is close to the ground and rests on a small wheel.

smoke oil. Air show pilots pump the oil into their engine exhaust to make the white smoke trail that traces their path through the sky. The smoke trail helps air show crowds follow their maneuvers.

Air show planes are built strong to take the stresses of aerobatic flying. The body of Wagstaff's plane has a steel tube frame that is covered with a skin of carbon fiber. This is a stiff, lightweight material used in top-quality tennis rackets and golf clubs. Other parts are made of Kevlar, a material used in bulletproof vests.

Patty Wagstaff prepares to fly her Extra 300XS. The bubble canopy will enclose the cockpit.

≡ Working the Controls

The controls are simple but sensitive. The control stick and rudder pedals control hinged surfaces on the airplane. These surfaces push against the wind to turn the airplane one way or another.

Pulling on the stick raises a hinged panel called an elevator at the back of the horizontal tail fin. Raising the elevator against the wind pushes the tail down, which raises the nose. Pushing on the stick raises the tail and pushes the nose down.

Moving the stick from side to side makes the airplane roll to one side or the other. It does this by moving a pair of hinged panels called ailerons. There is one aileron on the back edge of each wing. Pushing the stick to the left raises the left aileron and lowers the right one. The wind pushes against each aileron, forcing the left wing down and the right one up. The opposite happens when the stick is moved to the right.

The pedals control the rudder, a hinged panel on the vertical tail fin. It controls the side-to-side motion of the plane.

An airplane needs lift to fly, and its lift comes from its wings. As a wing slices through the air, its curved upper surface forces the air flowing over it to go faster than the air flowing under it. This causes a drop in pressure above the wing, and the air on the bottom pushes upward.

This only works when the air flows smoothly over the wing. If the wing moves too slowly through the air or the angle of the wing to the airflow becomes too great, the wing will stop producing lift. Pilots say the wing is stalled.

Power and Speed

The trick to recovering from a stall is to gain enough speed to get the air moving smoothly again. The powerful engine in Wagstaff's plane gives it a lot of thrust for quick speed.

"It accelerates like a rocket," she says. "It's capable of what I call hard-core, rock-and-roll aerobatics."[1]

The controls are so finely balanced that the airplane responds instantly to the lightest touch. An airplane so

Patty Wagstaff soars skyward in her Extra 300S.

Specifications for
Patty Wagstaff's
Extra 300XS

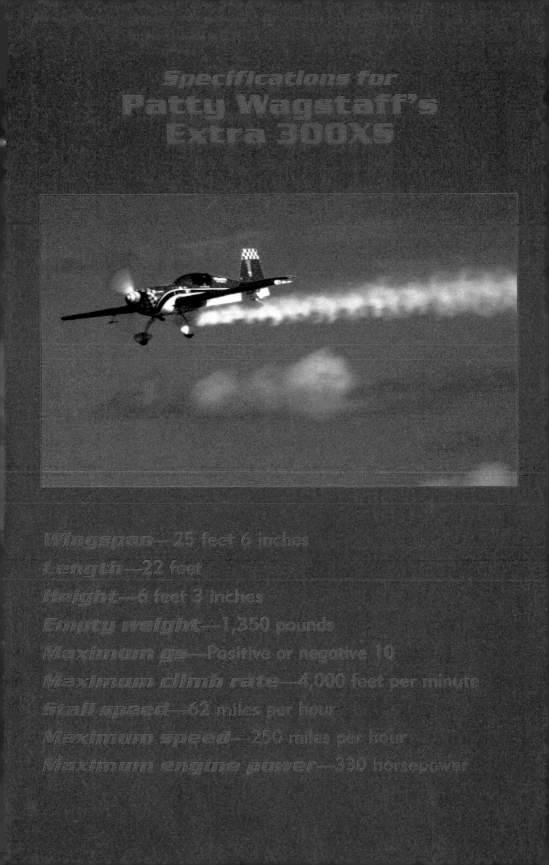

Wingspan—25 feet 6 inches

Length—22 feet

Height—6 feet 3 inches

Empty weight—1,350 pounds

Maximum gs—Positive or negative 10

Maximum climb rate—4,000 feet per minute

Stall speed—62 miles per hour

Maximum speed—250 miles per hour

Maximum engine power—330 horsepower

sensitive is not easy to fly, because it can quickly get out of control. But Wagstaff has flown it so much that it is like a part of her body. "You wear the airplane. You're not being flown around in something. You strap the airplane on. It plugs right into your brain," she says.

Wagstaff has owned several Extra airplanes. Her first was an Extra 260, the forerunner of the Extra 300 line. She flew an Extra 260 in 1991 when she became the first woman to win the U.S. National Aerobatic Championships. After winning the championships three times in a row, Wagstaff bought an Extra 300S, which allowed her to try even fancier maneuvers. She flew it until 1999, when she replaced it with the Extra 300XS, the most advanced model yet. Her Extra 260 is now on display in the National Air and Space Museum in Washington, D.C.

CHAPTER 3

A Physical Sport

Air show pilots are not daredevils. They know it is risky to fly wild maneuvers close to the ground, so they work hard to control the risks.

They practice at higher altitudes than they fly at air shows. This gives them room to recover if they make a mistake. And they practice constantly during the air show season. Besides the time it takes to master a new maneuver, Patty Wagstaff says aerobatic pilots need to fly often to keep their sense of where they are during tricky maneuvers.

"Any kind of flying, but especially this kind, requires one hundred percent focus," Wagstaff says.

Take Wagstaff's "snap roller" maneuver,

for example. She flies in a large circle while rolling the plane continuously. "If I don't do it every day, it makes me dizzy," she says. At one air show, she almost flew into the ground because she did not realize until the last moment that she was gradually coming down as she circled.[1]

Aerobatic flying requires more than good coordination. Although the pilot may be sitting in a cockpit, it is physically as tough as any athletic sport.

G Forces

Aerobatic maneuvers involve quick changes in direction. These quick changes push and pull at the body. The

The g forces that pilots feel during their maneuvers in the sky put much strain on their bodies.

amount of pushing or pulling is measured in units called gs. One g is the normal force of gravity. When you are standing on the ground or flying straight and level, you feel one positive g. If you do a headstand or fly upside down, you feel just the opposite—one negative g.

Wagstaff says her style of flying subjects her to up to ten positive gs and seven or eight negative gs. At ten gs, Wagstaff's normal weight of about 112 pounds feels like 1,120 pounds. Moving her arms takes tremendous effort. Heavy g forces also pull blood out of her upper body. If the blood were to drain out of her head, she could black out— lose her vision or lose consciousness.[2] Wagstaff fights it by tightening the muscles in her stomach and legs. This squeezes her blood vessels and prevents blood from draining into her lower body.

Negative gs do just the opposite. Blood surges into her upper body.

"The negative gs are really difficult," Wagstaff says. "Your eyes get swollen. . . . You really think your head's going to explode or your eyes are going to pop out of their sockets." Wagstaff says she built up to high negative gs slowly, and she stays used to it by flying negative-g maneuvers every day. "If you lay off for a week you don't stay used to it. . . . Some people get what's called the wobblies. Things start spinning."[3]

Wagstaff trains like an athlete. During the air show season, flying several times a day keeps her in shape. In the off-season, when her flying schedule is less intense, she works out in a gym with a personal trainer.

Air show pilot Sean D. Tucker signs his autograph for a fan.

After air show performances, pilots usually meet the air show crowd and sign programs or posters for fans. That is actually one of the hardest parts of air show flying, Wagstaff says. She might feel exhausted, she says, but she needs to appear at her best in front of her fans.

Would Wagstaff trade what she does for something easier? Hardly. "I like flying aerobatics because it combines everything I love—tumbling and floating, being upside down, freedom in three dimensions, travel and unlimited challenge—you can never know enough about it to completely master it."[4]

CHAPTER 4

Challenge in the Sky

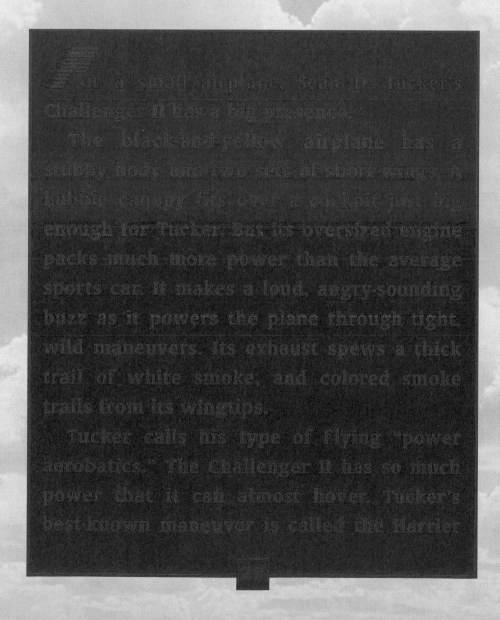

For a small airplane, Sean D. Tucker's Challenger II has a big presence.

The black-and-yellow airplane has a stubby body and two sets of short wings. A bubble canopy fits over a cockpit just big enough for Tucker. But its oversized engine packs much more power than the average sports car. It makes a loud, angry-sounding buzz as it powers the plane through tight, wild maneuvers. Its exhaust spews a thick trail of white smoke, and colored smoke trails from its wingtips.

Tucker calls his type of flying "power aerobatics." The Challenger II has so much power that it can almost hover. Tucker's best-known maneuver is called the Harrier

Sean D. Tucker puts his black and yellow Challenger II on its side. His powerful plane has two sets of wings, making it a biplane.

pass, named after a Marine Corps jet whose powerful engine can lift it straight up. The Challenger II cannot do that, but Tucker can make it come close. He pitches its nose up steeply and passes slowly by the crowd while its screaming propeller claws the air.

Such a quick, powerful airplane is not easy to master. "I call it the Challenger [II] because every time I get in the airplane, it reminds me to challenge myself in the sky," Tucker says.[1]

From the outside, the Challenger II looks like another popular airplane called the Pitts. Both are known as biplanes because they have two sets of wings. Tucker

Sean D. Tucker makes corncurls in the sky at Davis Monthan Air Force Base in Tucson, Arizona. The plane can spew white smoke from the exhaust and colored smoke from the wingtips.

learned aerobatic flying in Pitts biplanes, and he has always preferred them over other planes. "I think there's romance to biplanes" that appeals to crowds, he says. He also likes the tight maneuvers the Pitts biplane can fly because of its short, doubled wings.

≡ The Ultimate Machine

Tucker's first air show plane was a Pitts S-2S that he named Challenger. To get ever better performance as his skills improved, Tucker's Power Aerobatics team tore Challenger apart after every air show season and rebuilt it. When they did, they made changes to boost its power or make it more maneuverable.

Eventually, Tucker set out to get the ultimate air show machine. He contacted some of the best airplane craftsmen in the country. They worked up a design that combined the best qualities of the Pitts with those of other planes.

The result is the Challenger II, with wings based on one airplane, the body based on another airplane, and the tail on still another. Every part has been custom-built to achieve top performance.

While they were at it, the Challenger II's builders wired the plane for air show work. The wings have built-in control wires for smoke generators, fireworks launchers, and wing-mounted cameras.

The engine is a Lycoming aircraft engine that normally puts out up to 260 horsepower. Tucker hired a crew of engine rebuilders to beef it up so that it could crank out

Sean D. Tucker cuts a ribbon in a knife-edge pass with his Challenger II biplane. The custom-built plane was made for top performance.

another 120 horsepower—more than some small airplanes have altogether. Improving the exhaust system added another 10 horsepower.

The Challenger II made its air show debut in the 1997 show season. Tucker's team has continued to tweak the design to make it better.[2]

After a quarter century of flying biplanes, "I feel like it's a part of me," Tucker says. "I feel like the wings are my arms. . . . It flies like it's part of my brain. I just think about it and the airplane maneuvers that way."[3]

L. E. SMOOT MEMORIAL LIBRARY
9533 KINGS HIGHWAY
KING GEORGE, VA 22485

Specifications for Sean D. Tucker's Challenger II

Wingspan—19 feet 2 inches

Length—19 feet 1 inch

Height—6 feet 2 inches

Empty weight—1,160 pounds

Maximum gs—11 positive, 8 negative

Maximum climb rate—4,600 feet per minute

Stall speed—77 miles per hour

Maximum speed—250 miles per hour

Maximum engine power—390 horsepower

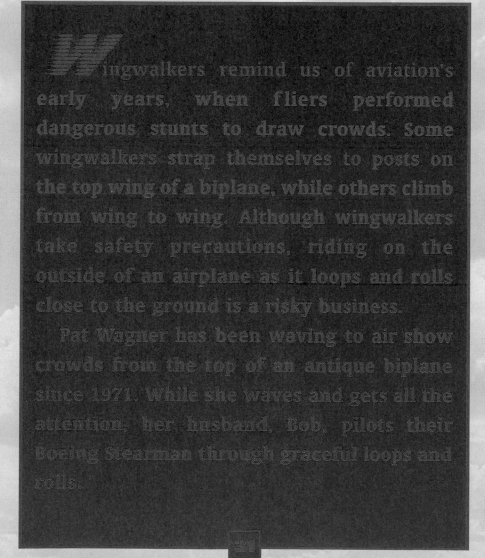

CHAPTER 5

Wingwalking

Wingwalkers remind us of aviation's early years, when fliers performed dangerous stunts to draw crowds. Some wingwalkers strap themselves to posts on the top wing of a biplane, while others climb from wing to wing. Although wingwalkers take safety precautions, riding on the outside of an airplane as it loops and rolls close to the ground is a risky business.

Pat Wagner has been waving to air show crowds from the top of an antique biplane since 1971. While she waves and gets all the attention, her husband, Bob, pilots their Boeing Stearman through graceful loops and rolls.

The Stearman is an old airplane. The Boeing Company built thousands of them as training planes for the armed forces in the 1930s and early 1940s. After World War II, the government sold off the trainers to civilian pilots. Big, tough, and maneuverable, the Stearman is still a popular air show airplane.

The Wagners' A75N1 Stearman was built in 1940. Bob, who is a mechanic as well as a pilot, made changes to it for Pat's wingwalking act. He more than doubled its engine power, from 220 horsepower to 450 horsepower. He strengthened the top wing where Pat stands. He also made the controls more responsive, to deal with the

Pat Wagner walks the wing while husband Bob pilots their Stearman.

change in balance to the plane and the extra drag of Pat's body against the wind when she stands atop the wing.

The most visible change is the large post mounted on the top wing. Braced by cables, the post has a seat belt and shoulder harness that Pat straps on to herself when she flies.

Actually, Pat calls herself a wing*rider* instead of a wing*walker*. "I don't move from the top [wing] to the bottom like some acts do," she explains.[1] Instead, she straps herself to the post before takeoff and remains there until after Bob has landed the Stearman and brought it to a stop.

Pat Wagner rides attached to the large post mounted on the top wing, while husband Bob flies their Stearman biplane.

Wingwalkers move about the plane while it is flying. For example, Kyle Franklin climbs between and on top of the wings of his father Jim Franklin's Waco biplane during their father-son wingwalking act. Tall and muscular, the younger Franklin looks built for the job. "I strap in when I'm on top of the wing, but the rest of the time I'm just holding on," he says.[2] His wild rides got even wilder in 1999, when his father mounted a jet engine to the bottom of the old biplane. The jet engine allowed the plane to soar skyward like a rocket—while Kyle stood atop the wing and waved like a bronco buster.

Risky Ride

Wingriding sounds safer than climbing around on the wings, but Pat Wagner says there are some risks. If Bob

Kyle Franklin wingwalks on his father's Waco. The jet engine is mounted under the airplane's belly.

scraped a wingtip or a tire blew on landing, it could flip the airplane over on top of her. If the engine quit, Bob might have to make a rough landing off the runway, and the same thing could happen. "I assume it would be fatal," Pat says matter-of-factly. But she says there is risk in everything. "You can be hurt falling down the stairs," she says.

What does it feel like to stand on top of an airplane that is looping and rolling through the sky? When strapped securely to the post, Pat says, "I feel like I'm part of the airplane." She can feel the effect of pushing through the air at speeds of up to 140 miles an hour. "I can tell the difference on my face and cheeks as the speed starts to change," she says. The wind pushes at her skin, and she can feel her cheeks flap as the speed builds up.

Pat wears goggles to protect her eyes from wind and bugs. In late summer, she can feel the smack of grasshoppers hitting her body.

Pat says the inverted pass—flying past the air show crowd upside down—gives her the strangest feeling: "Everything is pulling you down. You don't feel like you're on the airplane. You feel like you're hanging from it."

From her position, Pat can see in all directions. She loves to take in the sight of the crowd. "I have the best view of anybody at the air show. . . . Sometimes you can identify the kids and the people waving things."

That's when she's happiest, Pat says, "because then you know they're part of the show, too."

Specifications for Bob and Pat Wagner's A75N1 Stearman

Wingspan—32 feet 2 inches (upper);
31 feet 2 inches (lower)

Length—24 feet 10 inches

Height—9 feet 4 inches

Empty weight—2,800 pounds

Maximum gs—6 positive, 3 negative

Maximum climb rate—1,000 feet per minute

Stall speed—48 miles per hour

Maximum speed—207 miles per hour

Maximum engine power—450 horsepower

CHAPTER 6

Fast and Furious

While wingwalkers add an old-fashioned flavor to air shows, military teams add the thunder and fury of modern-day fighter jets.

Imagine yourself strapped into the cockpit of an F-16D Fighting Falcon. A gray oxygen mask covers your face, but your helmet sports the bright red, white, and blue of the U.S. Air Force Thunderbirds. In front of you, Thunderbird pilot Major Skip Johnson grasps the throttle and pushes it forward. The engine's power builds while Johnson holds the brakes.

"Smoke's on," he says. Outside, onlookers watch a cloud of smoke erupt from the back of the jet. It is the Thunderbirds' takeoff signal.

U.S. Air Force Thunderbird pilots perform at air shows around the country in their F-16s.

"Smoke's off," he says, releasing the brakes, and the jet starts to roll. It picks up speed rapidly. The force of acceleration pushes you back into your seat like a giant invisible hand.

"Here we go, Daddy-O. Right up into afterburner."

The afterburner boosts the engine's power. Johnson lifts the nose until the plane is off the ground, then levels it out. He raises the landing gear. Streamlined, the jet accelerates even faster, scorching down the runway centerline. By the time you reach the end of the runway, you are going 380 miles an hour.

"Ready to go vertical?" Johnson asks. He pulls back on the control stick and the ground disappears. All you see out front is blue sky. "Here we go. Goin' straight up," he says. Straight up like a rocket.[1]

Crowds Love Loud Jets

Nothing draws an air show crowd like a top military jet team. Fans love the sight of jets flashing across the sky in precise formations with a thunderous roar of engines. The Thunderbirds—the U.S. Air Force Air Demonstration Squadron—are the main attraction wherever they perform. They fly up to 88 air demonstrations every year between April and November. In the winter months they train new pilots at their home base, Nellis Air Force Base near Las Vegas, Nevada.[2]

The Air Force created its first military jet team in 1953. The Korean War was ending, and pilots were leaving the

Six U.S. Air Force Thunderbirds head into a straight climb over Nellis Air Force Base.

Air Force in large numbers. A jet team seemed like a good way to recruit new air cadets.

The team was first named the Stardusters, but the Air Force quickly changed its name to Thunderbirds. The thunderbird is a mythical Native American bird of prey. Its wings were said to make thunder when they flapped, and lightning flashed from its eyes. It was a fitting symbol for fighter jets.[3]

The Thunderbirds have flown several kinds of jets over the decades. "The policy has always been to demonstrate the [Air Force's] frontline fighter," says Staff

U.S. Air Force Thunderbirds fly in a tight-diamond formation at the 1999 United States Air and Trade Show.

Sergeant Bob Purtiman, the Thunderbirds' media relations chief in 2000.[4]

The squadron began flying an early version of the F-16 in 1982. In 1992, the Thunderbirds switched to the newer F-16C and F-16D. The F-16C is a single-seat model that the pilots fly in demonstrations. The D model is almost identical, but it has two seats.

A Thunderbird pilot and a mechanic use one of the F-16Ds to fly to an air show a day ahead of the rest of the squadron. They make sure everything is ready for the squadron's arrival. The squadron uses another F-16D to give rides to news reporters, celebrities, and politicians. The rides help the squadron get publicity and public support.

The pilots and their flashy F-16s are only a part of the Thunderbirds squadron. It includes about 140 people who do everything from office work to maintenance on the

Specifications for
F-16 Fighting Falcon[5]

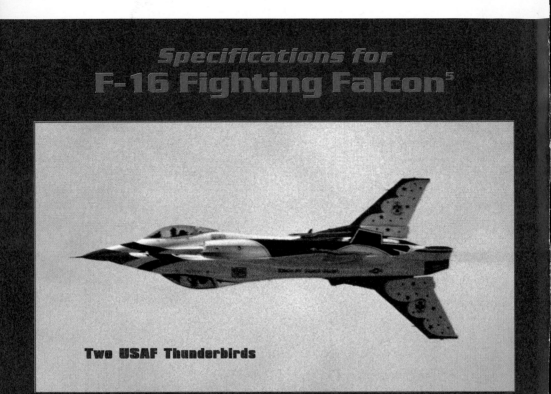

Two USAF Thunderbirds

Wingspan—32 feet 8 inches

Length—49 feet 5 inches

Height—16 feet

Empty weight—18,591 pounds

Maximum gs—9 positive

Maximum speed—1,500 miles per hour

jets. Between 50 and 60 people travel with the squadron to air shows. They fly in a big, C-141 cargo jet that carries spare parts, supplies, and maintenance equipment.

Thunderbird flight demonstrations include six airplanes. Four fly in a tight diamond formation to demonstrate precision. Two more fly solo maneuvers to show the maximum capabilities of the F-16.

The tight formations that the four formation jets fly are impressive, but the solo jets put on their own heartstopping maneuvers. In one pass, they fly head-on, barely missing each other as they roar past the crowd.

The squadron's best-known maneuver is called the high bomb burst. In this maneuver, four jets fly straight up in an X formation. High above the crowd they peel away from one another, each one looping backward. At the same time, a fifth F-16 shoots skyward up the middle of the formation, twirling to make a corkscrew-shaped trail of smoke.

Air show magazine publisher Dave Weiman says the Thunderbirds demonstrate more than military airpower: "Their performance is not only a demonstration of the military might of the United States, but also a demonstration of what can be accomplished through teamwork and individual self-discipline, hard work, and determination."[6]

Chapter 1. Strap In!

1. Author's flight with Patty Wagstaff, Avra Valley, Arizona, January 18, 1997.

2. Valdhere Films script, "Beachey, Lincoln—1966." National Aviation Hall of Fame, 1997, <http://www.nationalaviation.org/enshrinee/beachey.html> (January 6, 2000).

3. Dave Weiman, answers to author's questions via e-mail, January 11, 2000.

4. John Cudahy, answers to author's questions via e-mail, January 20, 2000.

Chapter 2. Rock-and-Roll Flying

1. Author interview with Patty Wagstaff, December 8, 1999.

Chapter 3. A Physical Sport

1. Author interview with Patty Wagstaff, December 8, 1999.

2. Author's note: This is known as g-induced loss of consciousness, or GLOC. The author experienced GLOC in 1989 in a 7-g turn during a flight in a U.S. Navy Blue Angels F/A-18. Fortunately, a Blue Angels pilot was flying the plane!

3. Author interview with Patty Wagstaff, December 8, 1999.

4. Patty Wagstaff, answers to author's questions via e-mail, January 19, 2000.

Chapter 4. Challenge in the Sky

1. Sean D. Tucker, answers to author's questions via phone message, March 21, 2000.

2. Sean D. Tucker Power Aerobatics, <http://www.poweraerobatics.com/air-planes.html> (December 18, 1999).

3. Tucker, answers to author's questions.

Chapter 5. Wingwalking

1. Author interview with Pat Wagner, February 15, 2000.

2. Conversation with Kyle Franklin, July 30, 2000.

Chapter 6. Fast and Furious

1. Author's flight with Major Skip Johnson, July 17, 1997.

2. Air Combat Command, "Thunderbirds," *USAF Fact Sheet*, September 1999, <http://www.af.mil/news/factsheets/Thunderbirds.html> (April 8, 2000).

3. U.S. Air Force Demonstration Squadron, "Thunderbird History: 1953 to Present," *USAF Demonstrations Squadron*, 1997, <http://www.nellis.af.mil/thunderbirds/history/history.htm> (December 7, 1999).

4. Author interview with Air Force Staff Sergeant Bob Purtiman, February 29, 2000.

5. Air Combat Command, "F-16 Fighting Falcon," *USAF Fact Sheet*, June 1997, <http://www.af.mil/news/factsheets/F_16_Fighting_Falcon.html> (April 11, 2000).

6. Dave Weiman, answers to author's questions via e-mail, January 11, 2000.

Glossary

aerobatic flight—An intentional maneuver involving an abrupt change in an aircraft's speed and/or direction.

aileron—A hinged surface on the back of a wing that is used to roll an airplane to one side or the other.

barnstormer—A pilot who travels around the country, usually to rural areas, giving air displays or selling rides.

biplane—An airplane having two sets of wings, one above the other.

canopy—A transparent covering over the cockpit of an aircraft.

cockpit—A space in an aircraft occupied by the pilot and sometimes other occupants.

control stick—A device that looks like a stick, usually mounted on the center of the cockpit floor. It controls the elevator and ailerons.

elevator—A hinged surface at the back of the horizontal tail fin that is used to control an airplane's up or down angle.

g—A unit of measurement for acceleration; one g is equal to the force of gravity at the earth's surface.

maneuver—Any deliberate departure from straight and level flight.

rudder—A hinged surface on the back of the vertical tail fin that controls an airplane's side-to-side motion.

stall—The condition when an airplane wing stops producing lift.

wingrider—One who rides in a fixed position on the exterior of an aircraft in flight.

wingwalker—One who rides or moves about on the exterior of an aircraft in flight.

Further Reading

Ayres, Carter M. *Pilots and Aviation*. Minneapolis: Lerner, 1990.
  *Describes the training and skills necessary to become a pilot
  and discusses other aviation careers.*

Lindblom, Steven. *Fly the Hot Ones*. Boston: Houghton Mifflin,
  1991.
  *Describes what it is like to fly eight different types of air-
  planes, including the Pitts biplane and the F-16 Fighting
  Falcon.*

Mackie, Dan. *Flight*. Niagara Falls, N.Y.: Durkin Hayes
  Publishing, 1986.
  *Describes various kinds of aircraft and aviation activities,
  including air shows.*

Yount, Lisa. *Women Aviators*. New York: Facts on File, 1995.
  *Describes women who have broken down gender barriers in
  aviation, from early air pioneers to astronauts.*

Internet Addresses

Experimental Aircraft Association. *EAA AirVenture*. © 2000.
  <http://www.airventure.org> (January 5, 2001).

International Council of Air Shows, Inc. *Air Shows*. © 1997–2000.
  <http://www.airshows.org> (January 5, 2001).

Patty Wagstaff Airshows, Inc. n.d.
  <http://www.pattywagstaff.com> (January 5, 2001).

Sean D. Tucker Power Aerobatics. n.d.
  <http://www.poweraerobatics.com> (January 5, 2001).

U.S. Air Force. *Air Force Thunderbirds*. n.d. <http://www.
  nellis.af.mil/thunderbirds> (January 5, 2001).

World Airshow News. n.d. <http://www.wanews.com>
  (January 5, 2001).

L.E. SMOOT MEMORIAL LIBRARY

3 1150 1002 6825 5

J   Gaffney, Timothy
629.13   R.
074   Air show pilots
Gaf   and airplanes

WITHDRAWN

L. E. SMOOT MEMORIAL LIBRARY
9533 KINGS HIGHWAY
KING GEORGE, VA 22485

L. E. SMOOT MEMORIAL LIBRARY
9533 KINGS HIGHWAY
KING GEORGE, VA 22485